My Grotesque Reflection Though

William Morton

Presentation by *BookLeaf Publishing*

Web: www.bookleafpub.com

E-mail: info@bookleafpub.com

ISBN: 9789363314320

First edition 2024

East Coast Team

Neglect the tired mind.
Neglect the mind that seeks the easy route.
Go and do what is progress.
Fight the urge to stay in a place that has little growth.
Wins aren't only when stuff is going the way they are.
Wins are when stuff isn't going the way they are but the individual has progression.

Money Strut

There is struggle that makes it hard to feel sympathy.
There is trauma that makes it hard to feel sympathy.
That is why the child's mind has so much value.
That child that grows is a revised reflection of the adult.
They see an unfiltered version that has no hardness.
The individual has a route that they can see the unfiltered reflection.
They can go and see that their ecosystem has no trauma and they can say what they need to say.
There is a character struggle in an individual.
They can't ignore the anger or negative emotions.
They seek the good but neglect the negative.

There is a course in these value systems.
The individual's character can get redeemed.
The individual that is good can lose their way but see good in the course.
The reputation is not who an individual is but character is who they are.

Stoic Men

The balance to seek pleasure but let it seek those that need to recognize what they desire.
Seek pleasure is to have little.
The poor man is not the man that has little but is the man that can desire much.
The struggle to say so much but to say so little.
Suppressed emotions.
Those who raise a poor man have failed as they put value on the toughness but not on the soft emotions.
The recognition of those soft feels are hard.

Gratitude Is The Attitude

Gratitude is what I woke up with.
I am grateful for those I love.
I am grateful to have love.
I am grateful for my health.
I am grateful for the gift of me.
That coincides with health.
The conditions are undefeated and my health can deteriorate.
I can have health but I am grateful for me.

Logic In The Office

I was so angry at myself for how much it hurt
when another says a quote that is hurtful.
A man is not supposed to feel this way.
What I've learned is that it's valid that it hurts.
These natural angry feelings that I have.
I can choose to let it hurt me.
What matters is me.

Comparison Poem

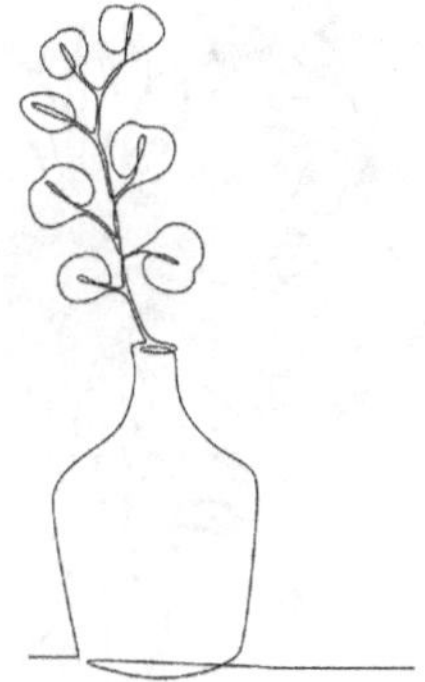

Comparison is the thief of joy.
Comparison is harmful to mental health.
Comparison makes dissatisfied egos.
Compete with the individual in the mirror.
The mind reflects what is looked at.
Comparison is an unfair condition that others
place on an individual.
Comparison is the thief of joy and the thought
that an individual is enough is relief.

The Land of Angry Men

In the land of angry men where they romp
around and play.
Laughter and others that encompass the day.
They have might to make their path.
Faced challenge with a hearty laugh.
In the land where angry men seem to flare.
There was those men who glare.
They huffed but there was a disguise in those
fiery eyes.
Stories and fears that was a sad hide.
The land of feels can get a sight.
These men are stoic but their minds eco faint in
the night.
The land of male normal thought.
Their feels should get the considered thought
that is ought.

Depression Whimsy

The ecosystem of whimsy which has sway.
The individual that was there was in constant disarray in the day.
The up of excited and the lull that was on the shore.
That individual could feel both satisfied and bore.
Moment of serene clarity like the sky.
Has anger and punches the mirror as if to ask why.
The go round of anger that is untamed
The individual is affected and is maimed.
So in the twists of thought there is whimsy to find.
The twists of both heart and in mind.

Paranoia Thoughts

The shadows linger and go in the lair.
Paranoia goes in the air.
The noggin which twisted thoughts play.
Veils of fear and cause sanity to pay.
The noggin which in its way is a twisted joy.
They say what they say in reassurance but it's the mind's ploy.
They creep and hide.
They make individuals say "act like a man" but they neglect what's inside.

Client On The Couch

The thoughts twist and twirl with despair.
They play fog on reason and tangle with care.
They say stuff in shadows and laugh in gloom.
They say stuff in the midst of the fray.
Gnaw at sanity's way.
They look and scare at the corridors of thought.
The face which is now a facade is wrought.
There is glimmer.
The mind can only carry so much or it can get dimmer.
The only way to get out is to have reassurance in the day.

Respected Women

The land so vast and look at the demographics of him but not of her.
They do the jobs and do them with reduced pay.
The man is the man but the woman makes the day.
Yes they are so nice and so kind.
They care for men and are such the find.
The boardroom to the kitchen is what they see.
Respected now and respected on a whim.
Respect goes to respected women.

This Condition

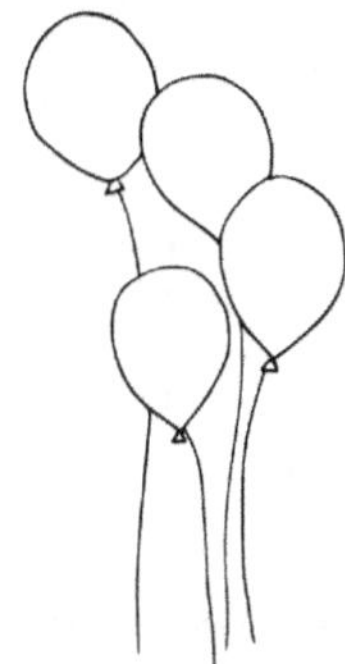

The health condition that impacts those that are affected.
This condition is characterized by emotions and profound struggles in maintaining the balance of self.
Individuals that have this condition face challenges that make it hard to interact with stuff.
There's the emotional turbulence.
Their emotions can shift.
It's not uncommon for individuals to feel emptiness.
Interpersonal interactions are part of this conditions effects.
The fear of rejection is there though the individual needs connection and support.

Whinging Tangents

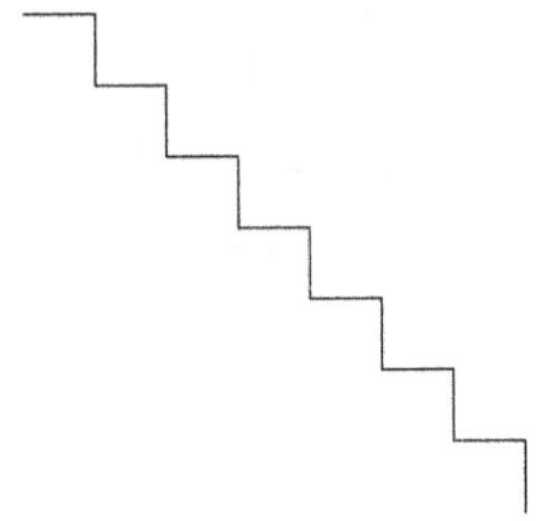

Those complaining sprees referred to as
whinging tangents.
Frustrating to those around.
Merit understanding and consideration.
Recognize that complaining is from unmet needs
and frustrations.
They resort to vocalizing there dissatisfied ways
to get validation.
It's a cry for help.
A way that expressed what it should.
Whinging provides an outlet for emotions.
They vent their frustrations as a mechanism.
Complaining is togetherness among individuals.

Those Thoughts

The anxiety that manifests in ways.
Those challenges that are hard to make rations.
Situations that are subject to neglect to others
can cause anxiety to individuals.
This constant alertness makes it hard for tasks.
The features of this condition is the fears of
specific objects or situations.
There are obsessive and compulsive thoughts.
These rituals and routines that soothe anxiety but
are disrupt others.
Panic is an occurance.
There is an interplay of anxiety and fear.
Those that are affected are those that can soothe
what they can.

Those Halcyon days

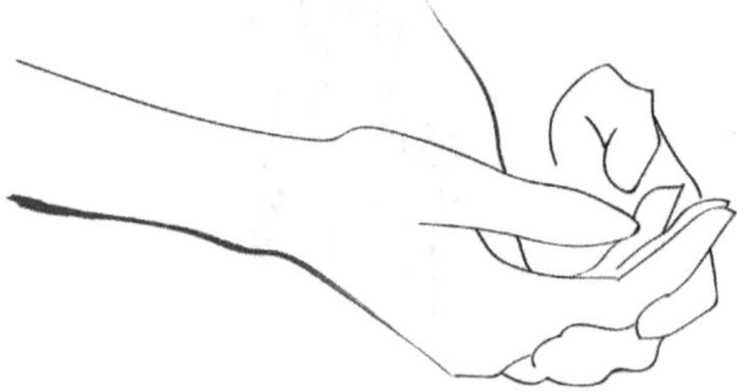

Those halcyon days which are those moments in the past that seem enveloped in a glow of memories.
The pace is fast in occupations.
These memories are a way of reminiscence.
They are a way to maintain identity.
They narrate the part that is integral.
These moments that the individual was glad makes it clear that that joy can get attained.
Those memories are selected but they show the joy and not the sad parts.
The thought of the halcyon days are profound and are looked at as echos of the past.
They show the joy that was there and is there.

Women of Color

In the curls that are tough and are part of their head hair.
They flaunt their strands and their flares.
Their natural glow blooms with a vibrant hue.
Their hair shines in view.
Women of color are here and they are to not yield.
Women of color in sports or women of color who are regular.
They are part of the day and men of varied color should act as their shield.
Women of color should love their natural hair.
Women of color are of value and can not compare.

Rejection

The fear of rejection.
Not a passing concern but an overwhelming presence.
Not a scenario but is their situation.
The feeling goes unrecognized.
Casual response can cause emotional reactions.
The need for reassurance.
The individuals acutely can see their actions.
Rejection is not who they are.
They need support on ways to reinterpret others.

Adolescence To Adulthood

The lands where the child has their view.
They look at the sky of which is blue.
They go from the child to the adult and such is a chore.
The thought of tasks and burdens are a bore.
The chore of adulthood is a bore and the mind needs a door.
So if the child can go into an adult and that child mind can stay.
Oh the place that child can go and the place that child can play.
Adolescence is to explore.

The thoughts twist and twirl.
The blurred quotes that act as notes
Noise that is noise of which the mind is not poised.
The clatters which seem to saunter but are blurred yet clear.
The voice of the mind is what is to fear.
Here to there and reassurance of care.
That noise and that voice is what can appear.
The mind is a canvas.
The moments of clarity.
Echos of fears and hopes.

Validation and Acceptance

Acceptance is compassion.
Recognition and respect.
Validation is if an individual is valued.
Validation that an indiv matters.
Acceptance is maturity.
An individual is who they are and they accept that.
Maturity is acceptance.
I can look at my reflection.
I can look in the mirror.
I am enough.

www.ingramcontent.com/pod-product-compliance
Lightning Source LLC
LaVergne TN
LVHW020546160826
845677LV00015B/4228

9789363314320